East of a Cold Red Sun

Shatara liora

Δ

First Edition

Printed in USA

ISBN-13: 978-1541099777

ISBN-10: 154109977X

For Joyce Marie.
who is love, personified.

Table of Contents

Table of Contents

skin

elderly matriarchs say
protect your yoni
eat your vegetables
get up early on Sundays

I say
I am mourning
I am damaged
there is no garden here

they say
it is just wisdom
piercing skin
growing
you've got vulnerability
and love lost rattling
inside your bones

you'll be just fine
surely, you'll be a wife
and not a jezebel

oh yes,
a mother
fat and healthy
heartbroken, nurturing

god forgive you, if you decide to be lost
and beautiful
all at once

the flower's eye

break me to halves
then to pieces
then to seeds
and plant me in a lover
whose body is earth
and hands are of water

leave me there
where I can taste the sun
in my mouth

vines that stretch

you may ask where
did this wisdom come from

my spirit tastes old

it has ripened like low hanging fruit below my breasts
it has grown branches as long as my arms
it burns it cools it writhes
a turmoil in my stomach
yet it calms like holy basil in tea

this wisdom   it grew
from mourning wars
within my skin

it came from making love when there was none to be found
it came from looking at my body in disappointment
while friends laughed and played guitars in the hallway
it came from fear and anxiety and trauma and abuse
it came from insecurity about not measuring up to wives and virgins
and mistresses with eyes like lagoons and roses for nipples

it came from being high on life then spiraling down
to dark places and having to crawl out on my own

it came from the one who held me yet had to go
it came from holding back tears while I allowed myself to tremble instead
it came from bruising my hands when I patched up my own
sides, because they were leaking sorrows

wisdom kept repeating itself   planting itself
kept throwing me around till I could laugh and cry and surrender

creating nations

touch me like I am new again
as if I am the one you always wanted
and our love languages are no longer
immigrants in the other's land

touch me as if I am a virgin
in all white
on a wedding day
walking barefoot up the aisle through the grass
a wreath around my hair like an angel
dying to make love to blues music in the kitchen

touch me like I am slipping through your hands
puncture me with love
pluck my petals and breathe me in through your mouth

touch me
make us new again
I want to be where you plant your seeds
let me create nations
just for you

texture

if only her little hands had touched kinky-haired dolls
as her delicate psyche formulated ideals
of beauty and femininity

if only western ideals had not ruptured her
did not weigh so much
did not make her feel she should pray
for blue eyes and porcelain skin

if only society
had put her on a pedestal too

if only she had not been taught
to despise
her own richness
and worship
any texture but her own

if only her scars did not still fester
for only the salves she herself makes
soothes them

unrequited

I've always wondered why you never loved me
I balanced and stretched myself thin
I adorned my hands and softened them to touch you like a wife
I patiently waited when you traveled and made new homes
to show you that I could wait just like a wife

I wore white on sundays
turned myself into lace on fridays
even learned new recipes
I put fresh flowers in vases next to prayer books
to show I had integrity like a wife
and the home of a wife

I lay with you into the morning
let you devour me as if I was your wife
till your spirits were buried into my linens
but you still could not love me
though I sacrificed like a wife

when you arose small pieces of my hair stuck to your face
and you smelled odd—like oak trees
as if a husband who tended the yard

but you were only searching for your boots
by the door
while my love hung stretching
like a whore

traumas

In your sleep, fear crawls in your hair
and on your lips
leaving it dry and bitter to greet the morning

you awake
unrested
logical thought processes swell and burst
you jump with nausea

disillusioned is an understatement
because you will never be the same
or see people as good
or the world in color

because you have been violated
beaten
struck
touched
left

you remember when you blended in with the world
ignorance was bliss

but now your thoughts—like scissors—have carved out
burdensome memories
and made a mural of pain

with normalcy lost there is healing to do
trust must be sewn back into your skin

and those murals reset
a world of color to relearn

wells

I hope you find a love that tastes like lavender
and blooms in your hands

love that wakes up early
and fetches water

love that makes you feel like yourself

evolved

hypervigilance

wreckage in my stomach
remembering hands
that felt like war
violating me
for so long that
when I finally wept
my tears were shards of glass
piercing
cutting
after what was once supposed to be love
turned to menacing ghosts

bitterness eats my body
grief sits in layers on my lap
while every footstep outside sounds like
thundering shattering asphalt

I jump at every sound

fear lines my mouth even when silence surrounds me
I am cracked along the edges
with burdens of shame

nightmares in my belly
run amok around my organs
as if an animal in the wild

once was all it took to have a lover made of wars
to alter me

to ruin me
to teach my body how to heal itself

ancestors

the ancestors are not pleased
they do not recognize us
they call out frantically from the sand

they see our self-hate
and shattered mirrors
glistening under a rejected sun

they see a plan deviously devised and sold
to a people who believe they are free
but are still prisoners to themselves
and blind to their own history

the ancestors turn and weep and wail
we do not recognize them

their hair grew upward like crowns adorned with
rubies emeralds and lotus blossoms
we do not recognize them
because their history is not in our books

their languages not on our tongues

veils

you make weeping willows stand upright toward a cracking sun
after centuries of goodbyes there was a hello
it quenched me
loosened my hardened clay

grind me down
mold me
to fit into your hands
so I'll be wanted again and again

show me how women of faraway cultures
rise above barren lands
and heavy hearts

your love is heavy
like those veils ancient women wove
for virgins with flowers in their hair

within the wreckage

the absence of a father made me an easily targeted gazelle
my childhood of ongoing travel in foreign lands gave me
separation anxiety and a yearning to know
what home smelled like
my petite frame lacked womanhood expectations
and made me watchful and empathetic
my hair- not meeting society's expectations- made me shifty and tired

the traumatic stories I was told
made me grateful but damaged

watching my mother work and try to keep us safe beneath
her bosom
made me brave but fearful

made me feel that every woman's truth was strength wrapped in pain
it made me feel as though men were like ships

I never went out of my way to make them stay, I never thought they were meant to

women

strong women are seen as big unpleasant buildings
blocking views of beautiful parks and oak trees
a threat to order
a temple that is no longer sacred
pompous, unfeminine, and bulky
a thorn in the side
stained couches

the world uses strong and independent interchangeably
taking away the beauty of both
robbing the quietly strong that cleans floors while pots boil over
with love that weighs more than a century
and stays

while the other, independent, busies herself
because her sides leak sorrows without companionship
but because she is of substance and intellect
she can survive
she has not denied love is what she seeks
despite societies' accusations

what will be done to the strong woman?
a sore thumb of society, they say
she failed to stay in her role
she failed to only be her womb

she built herself like a ship
that could carry you if the tide goes too high and took you under its belly

don't you see she faces the same fate of the weak woman,
that the world has failed to see does not exist

a lover made of wars

I want to put your pain in a rocket
fill in the gaps of your past that made you grey and full of ashes
I want to command the universe to fill your wounds with empathy and handpicked herbs

I want to get on my knees and cry until my breath is heavy and dragging
maybe even hold you like a child
I know I would feel your pain aching in my fingertips
I'd keep asking if it was over yet

but if the pain was meant to reside and breathe within you
I'd want to dissolve you
I'd want to send you upstream into nothingness
I would hope my abandoned heart would forget and dismantle you,
like it has always had to do when the world tilts and throws its daggers

I want to put your pain in a rocket
I want to fill in the empty spaces of you
that are void

and if you must accept a fate of being a carrier of burdens
and addictions that turn you into stone

I do not want your memories stuck between my fingers
or echoing throughout my veins

making tribes fall

my skin is so dark
it pulsates and radiates like gold

touch me

my hair greets the sun effortlessly
it softly coils to and fro
it delicately sleeps against my scalp once it's waters dry

touch me

my lips are full as though they might explode
because they are full with ancient wisdoms
and daffodils

kiss me

my curves tell stories of Queens who ruled tribes
and made Kings fall to their knees
that is why the world refuses to see the beauty in me

they are afraid

just to touch me

and understand

sacred

I have had breathtaking love once before but the universe
swallowed it and spit it out into the eye of an abyss
to see if I could survive once it left

now I have risen - and the memory lingers
patiently
chasing itself

and now I will not settle for mediocre love

i will not allow anyone to make me prove I am magical
for i was flung from the sands and waters and the ribcage
and it is already evidently so

you must find me
then handle me gently in your hands
even when things are wild
I need to feel your tight grip
on the small of my neck
telling me ships were meant to return after long journeys

because you have tasted love once too
and your memory also chases itself
again and again

just like me
you've sat on its terrain
you know how it behaves
you've heard it laugh behind your back

so now you will not settle for mediocre love either
and you don't need proof that I am what I am
a spirit
a body that warms you
a throat with words climbing up

divine

songs

don't dance with me when my favorite song plays
because if you leave
the song will then puncture me with holes
the nostalgia will then grow teeth
maybe even claws

don't make my favorite food
or stare through me while we eat at restaurants
because if you walk away
I will lose my appetite

why would anyone want to become a shell of who they once were
all because of a memory
attached to things we need to survive

rosebuds

I cut my hair
and became a woman I never knew
an amazon
a warrior
I adorned my short locks with beads and ribbons made from sea moss

I broke the sole of society's heavy boot that hovered over me
with its shadows

I was free
an organic version of me
authentic and bold

love flowed from my spirit
back into itself
breaking up clouds

I could be seen again
an unfiltered goddess in my own right

a black butterfly
breaking chains

I let the rain fall over me
and watched my hair become rose buds

story of sandpaper

there was a woman like sandpaper. she was odd to look at - like a slanted hill with slanted trees that couldn't balance themselves. her tongue was like a snake, slithering and hurling insults - as if she knew so much.

while I sat having a cigarette and moonshine she told me I was dumb.

she was always getting on my case like she was perfect - like no one had ever drowned her in love and left her humiliated. she had no bad habits so she was sandpaper. no vices to smooth her.

she raised all of her younger siblings but never had children of her own. she had become hardened - hard as glass. and piercing. i imagined balling her up and throwing her onto the pavement so she would crack into a million pieces. then she would be like me.

we would sit on the balcony and I would watch her from the corner of my eye. she even sat in her chair unpleasantly - like a guard dog.

she wasn't pretty. and when she was mean to me I wanted to tell her so, but she knew it. her whole life, she knew it.

in the middle of the night if she heard me whimper she would slide into my bed and hold me until I stopped shaking - cooing softly like a mother bird. her breath was so close, it was food.

she showed me how a woman's love can be hard - hard but forgiving.

on those nights I could look through her like I was pressing my face against a screen door
– but
i would always stay inside.

isn't that something?

cities

there will be cities you can't revisit
because the memory of me will flood your mouth
like melon water
and you will curse my name

i am not sorry

manifest

the sun greeted me this morning
it dried up the remnants of yesterday that found its way onto the balcony
I meditated in the living room underneath bamboo blinds
thankful for the light from the east

the sun opened up the sky
there was no trace of storm clouds that blew black roses
on my doorstep days ago

there was a sense of peace
ideas were unfolding
my spirit danced

there was love in the balance
there was warmth in the ground

there was stillness in my heart
that pulled me through the night

there was no sorrow lingering into the new day
there was only sun
and my outstretched arms

thankful for the light from the west
thankful for the light from the creator

ache

love's liqueur spills from me -

creating puddles around my feet

art lines the walls but the windows still throb and ache

memories grow legs and crawl into corners of the room

they ask me to dance while I clean melancholy from underneath my nail beds

drown

You ask me to visit you
the problem is, you only want to see me without clothes
and that would be fine if you were willing to read the languages on my skin

but you are not

I want to walk up mountains and follow lightning bugs to lakes or gardens that don't end
I want to pick fruits and watch plum water fall from your mouth when you laugh
and run for cover when the rain comes
I want to cut vegetables and put on old records when we find our way back

but you
only want to dig your hands into my skin
impatiently
you want to cover my mouth with yours
and make me moan
to silence me
about running from rain and picking fruits

but I am
not a shallow puddle you jump into just to watch water fly

I am an ocean of eyes that see and a body that wants to be full
I will drown you

so I had better stay home

cruel

I am afraid of the world
because of the people in it

they are cruel
without noticing

without seeing how they reek of it

there are people who are cruel
in low places
as well as high

this world, where some people must run from their homes in order to be free
where children cry out for clean water
ravished by famine

I am angry at the world, because some traditions mutilate women
just to rob them of pleasure
and marry them at eight years young
and stone them if one person mutters she is impure

this world, where buildings crumble on top of innocent people
in the name of religion and hate

where people despise others who do not look or talk like them
where outward racism is discussed
but not the worst of all: institutional racism

it impacts generations
causes loss of value of self
and trickles down only
to statistics

a world where the children ignore the elders
and morality is lost

a world where there are people abusing animals
mutilating them out of anger and sociopathy

we live in a society where cruelty can smile

yes, that is the world we live in today

and I am angry
but mostly, I am afraid

softly

if you love someone despite their flaws
it means your mind has filled in their cracks
with what you hope them to be
imagined they could be
despite who they really may be
ointment on a scar
of an unknown source

in a tiny room with lips on your neck
nibbling and speaking softly
to a body that drips
begs and coils
on and on

of what it wishes you to be

—oh the risk of trust

water bearer and fish

you're like pollen
and it is spring
my throat is dry and your name swims underneath my tongue

I have ignored the pangs in my stomach
and my weakened organs that feel like they've been wrung out—
left out like old wash rags

my body is exhausted from my inability to cope with having to release you
to let you go

I am burning sage
I have healing stones along the walls

so I must rise up like the moon
to drive the dark away

that old boring heartache that will become sticky sweet
if you don't pull it up from the roots of grieving soil

ghosts of men

I wish I was the type of woman who could say
please don't go
without pride getting stuck in my throat
like tough winter fruits
and fear exploding in my stomach

keeping your love vague will only leave you
grasping

paint

I am not letting you go because I want to
I am letting you go because I must
because you are euphoria
a bottomless pit

you have a touch that makes me warm and high
the type of love that will make me think about throwing it all away
and I am in no position to throw away
things

I am letting you go because your colors change
from yellow to red to black, then back again
without explanation
without you understanding the effects of such a thing

a tornado
a tsunami

you've broken everything you have ever gotten your hands on, they say
I am still dizzy from the fall of 1000 feet

I am letting you go
because you have broken me in half
and now anhedonia
lays with me
climbing up my elbows and cutting into my skin
I can taste blood in my mouth from the wounds
but it tastes like muscadines

and now I have to move on
try again with someone I do not know
I have to pretend to not be this fragile, damaged thing

I have to get you off of me
all of these changing colors you left in my aura
and in my windows

I have to be a blank canvas
If someone else will ever have me

dove

there
in the corridor
is a girl

you must have fallen from the sky?
you sweet little dove
so fancy but so empty

why don't you open your mouth and speak?
is your language creamy and cursive?

has your beauty silenced you?
has the world told you who you are
and you believed them?

does your mind sit silently because you uprooted
all the blossoms from your heart—
the blossoms of who you could have been?

join me in the wild

I have had moments of fear that I did not know could exist

there are things in life that can alter you
changing the sweet tunes in your spirit
to melancholic hums
there are traumas that cannot be undone
abuse that cannot be unseen

but I am not here to run
or to be afraid of things that are inevitable like death or love
or circumstance

there are things in life we must meditate on

we were not meant to live in fear or to run
not if we believe in a Creator
the one who can diminish our fear
and dismantle it with His fist

or if we believe in a watchful universe that will hear us cry out
and protect us
manifesting karma to those who are cruel
those who have tried to devastate us
violate us

so I will stand here
and what will be will be

I will not live in fear because unspoken things have happened to me in my life

I will live because of it

braille

I fear that my love is so abundant it will break you at the seams
because my vulnerability is now my strength and not my weakness
I am happy and full

there are no seeds of sorrows planted here
so my hands wait to hold you and trace fingers down your skin
as if braille is waiting there
my legs beg to rest upon you in the evening

could you handle a love that feels this strong
what about if it came on slow, like a soft gust of wind

I fear that when my mouth touches yours you will taste my truth
and my truth is pure and honest
it tastes like rain falling

I want our love to hide with each other
find a corner of its own and tangle itself up

love swims in my eyes and it is so unfair for me to look away
and not let you see

even if I am a piece of lint in your pocket

insignificant

and by your side

indigo zen

drinking warm white tea infused with exotic fruits
that nurture my insides like balm
in the afternoons I set my cup on a dark wood table
next to an indigo lamp that softly buzzes and ticks
and In those moments I close my eyes and find myself
running
running
running
through flower fields
that stretch
far
far
far
and I am twirling, letting nature lick my hands
and it is fading fast
because only in the mind
can the world be so peaceful

for miles

jezebel

she always had lovers
men's chests to lay her face against
for her, it felt like home
i imagine her insides
were decorated
but
echoed like hallways

hallways with old pictures hanging up
sheer linens like ghosts over lights
candles burning that would fall over
and catch it all on fire

then all her lovers would come
with buckets of water
leaving their wives sleeping in their beds

yoni water

when will you learn that your heart and yoni are stitched together
you laugh as though you want and can do what the men do
but are you not also made of flowers and glass
when you're crushed and shattered into pieces
how will you explain yourself

do you not know the universe made you to be delicate and rooted in soil
it made you to survive hot and cold
love and grief
lovemaking and childbirth

you are not made me be stitched and unstitched
like some rag doll
with yarn for hair
and a smiling open mouth
that doesn't speak

everyone should not know
the inside of your legs
and its formulas
such as
how your waters land
and how deep they run

everyone already knows water sustains life
and women have water and blood

so when you try to be like the men
you cannot
your body is too brilliant

fathers

he had a daughter
with eyes like his

his hands became soft
his feet slower and patient
wrinkles around his eyes deepened
with worry of karma

worry of tears staining
her soft yellow blouse

wear the mask

you do not care that I am here
I have already loved you
more than you've ever desired
a thousand lifetimes worth
of love
I am nothing new
I am what you had when you were
hunting
when your words were fresh
as lemons
saying things like
you are beautiful
and
can I get to know you
and
have you ever been in love?

So here I am
thinking of
my insignificance
my ring
the mask
a man who hunts and only loves
a while

who strays
then loves only when I am all packed up

patience choking at my feet

he loves so much,
then

when we touch

don't it make my brown eyes black
don't it make my body become flower beds
made of the oldest bones
you've ever known

don't it make my brown eyes black
to know a love of substance
a love of profoundness
the most utopic place you've ever swam

a love with crevices to hold your limbs and tuck away your truths find earth and silence

I went out today to look for simplicity
for silence
and inner dialogue
and found the earth has much to offer
open sky that leads
stones that reveal
leaves that whisper secrets of healing

and I plucked flowers
and tossed them into the waters
to lay in
and simplicity rested upon me
kneading my body
writing poetry into my skin

dismantled wombman

society says that I am not beautiful
because not only is my skin dark
but I am black

I am black,
therefore, I am not smart
or elegant
or magnificent

society says I am nothing anyone wants to be
not even other people who share my color
but refuse to be black

society believes even before I speak
I am disregarded
abandoned
ruined
incapable
low

society thinks I should never speak
because if so
I am aggressive
masculine
intimidating

society says I should hate myself
and those who are like me
because they are of no value
because only one of us can succeed
only one of us can be beautiful

society has
forgotten
I am
pure rain falling from the sky
soft florets in your hands
algorithms you cannot calculate
bones older than earth

I do not break.

phoenix clichés

I didn't want to be a cliché
a phoenix burning

but there I was
rising
emerging from fire
wisdom for eyes

survival roaming in my blood
creating lines in my palms

a story to someday tell daughters
whose lips had become raw with love

the beginning

there is something about the way love shows up when you're least expecting it. something about how it feels when it first arrives. how it tastes. how it turns your breath to song notes. you spread yourself on your bed when the lover is not there, to get the scent close enough to enter your pores. their voice lingers along your ears and patiently sits on your ear lobes. their presence stands in the doorway even when not there. your insides call for them. with the lover near, you feel nourished, in the same way you are burned by the sun and cooled by the rain.

the honeymoon.

the new sweet caresses feel sticky sweet like southern humidity. the love is like nectar, feeding you as though you were starving and never knew it.

deserts

my anxiety clings to me like wet clothing
society does not understand
we are meant to go slowly
patiently
with empathy leading our paths
to a neutral harmony
to reveal oasis
and eyes that acknowledge
our deficits and fears

we have failed ourselves

we must learn patience
we must learn love
forgiveness
trust
and healing from the inside

east side story

why do films exclude when love shreds you
and leaves gaping holes that will never close?

does life not imitate art?

does life not in one moment throw thorns in your side
and in the next moment surround you with
beautiful big red moons?

do they not want to show
sometimes the moons never come
and the dark stays still?

it is still and you can't even breathe out the sadness
you'd rather fold over in grief than breathe

jewelry box

now I no longer know if the man who remembers what I said three weeks ago was sent from the universe to love me or if his fingertips itch to dismantle me later. using his good memory to appear soft only to strike me later. and all I will remember was how sweet it was, that he remembered. and I will only see how his eyes lit up remembering. and there I am. a woman dismantled. who only remembers what he remembered. and it keeps me there and in love. wasting away. remembering.

mosaic of youth

I used to go out of my way
to prove that I was
not
exactly
what I was

it was exhausting to be young and seeking

and no one reminded you of yourself

the clutches of you

where there's smoke and downpours of rain, there's you
where there's trains to san francisco
and dancing in the street, there's you

where there's bars with city views and conversations with strangers about love
there's you

you make unfamiliar places familiar

you cling more than my own skin

submit

peace King
when you speak
my knees submit
my womb expands
because you have dandelions between your teeth
penetrating the air I breathe
pollen
royalty
forgotten pharaoh
even if you say off with their heads
or I need you, my rib
i look away in adoration of your power

it is effortless

renaissance harlem

I imagine
if I was ever to go to Harlem
I'd see ghosts
and hear music playing
underneath concrete

literature on roses
that came through the sidewalks

jazz in the night air
knocking on my hotel window
with drinks and stories
that leave the blues and its aromas
in my coat
for the ride home

cotton hummingbird

I imagine a voyage of abomination
the sweat
the blood
sliding down wood that groans
into an unforgiving ocean

I picture pitch black skin
sweat, hot as tar
balled up hair underneath dirty rags
eaten up by salt water

cloths for dresses
stitched by swollen hands
hot as stinging wasps
and angry sun

I see a woman's womb shifted out of place
singing songs that hide within trees

I see cracked ground where only cotton and despair grows

and I weep into my hands

the black bird sings

joyce marie

the only thing that can do the same thing

the setting sun does to the sky:

my mother.

delicately.

soothing everything

with ragged edges

in this world

like balm
like honey
or soft rain
in an orchard

love personified.

when you remember

some memories we must scrape from

our skin and throw into the fire.

turning

you do not get to invade my space or my body
without me being yours and you mine
do you think that your presence alone should get you what you want from me?

your ego is an atrocity.

and you may very well disappear
but I know you will never be fed
because you only know how to starve

you do not know
the work involved
in being full

so you take bites
out of hollow women

women still finding themselves
who let your ego
rub against their bodies
until it feels raw

and then they become me.

firewater

you do not know how to love things that love you back

you reincarnate sadness

and drown in it in firewater

what traumas left you void?

what makes you want to burn along the insides?

whose absence made you afraid of having someone present?

notes on the walls

I do not want a love that comes attached to strangling roots
I want love from the ends of the earth
running wild with second chances
released
and rebirthed

panting and breathing wildflowers

bitter fruits

here comes the scalding moon again
creating light where there is none
putting splinters in the sky
having her way with the tides

creating silhouettes

making us miss what we lost
making us remember how great it was

to have a hand grasp you
while you slept
and pull you close

love entwined and simmering softly on the spine of the bed

daughters of rolling stones

take me to places where vineyards grow wildly
where we can make love and eat fruits
where mountains beckon us

where our pasts can no longer keep up with us
and we are no longer afraid of things we can't predict

take me to where I can bury my feet into earth
and soak up its healing

we don't have to be nomads
we only have to be brave

wallpaper

there is a suitcase on the back porch and regrets rising like smoke from ash trays
the same song is playing and it is lingering between the blinds

and there you are –
sitting in the corner of the shower
rocking back and forth
trying to remember the night before, but it escapes you

well, your addictions got the best of you
and you tore down the wallpaper
with angry hands
almost like you were breaking bones

to hear you cry could make the sky fall
anyone would forgive you

even hell would send you back

there is a suitcase on the back porch
and a red bird in the trees
there are words on my tongue that taste soggy
they've grown mold

I am trying to forget
the addictions that seeped down
cracking wallpapers we picked out on a sunday

I can never return

love medicine

we fell in love in the dark corners of a place where only sinners go
and we laid our sins next to each other

and I knew you were the type that would never let me leave
because you never had anything worth having
you've ravished the best things you've ever known

I would become medicine
and you would be incapable of harm
because through me, empathy has sunk inside of you

you'd be healed of darkness while here
and we would have to pack up our sins and move on
separating eventually-
because yours came back like a dark hot tar
pulling you down the holes in the pavement

and I would become numb forever
reeking of love medicine

towers

I am trying to remember nights from paris
but I have never been there
I have been sleeping all alone
and I have gotten quite delusional
as my insides dry up
from not having a body to fall into

I am trying to remember nights from vegas
walking on stiff desert heat at 4 am
trying to seem welcoming

lovers calling from the windows
cards on the floors

and I realize I can have as many lovers as I want
while I wash away thoughts of us
in pools with pink water

if only I was built for these types of cities
where love is blinking lights
towers
goodbyes
and rolling stones

never ending

the daggers of our past try to twist after they strike us
but why do we let our past in anyhow?
why do we not bury them or send them into the eye of an abyss?

our past can ruin everything we could be –
by making us feel we are always supposed to be
what was behind us
what is no longer

and what is no longer

is powerless

good morning king

every time you call and say goodnight I wonder
if you will call to say good morning
I would rather hear your voice after
you have been unaware of the things around you
unconscious
creating visions you cannot understand

I would rather hear your voice rough and rugged
as if you have just been on a long journey
and you've seen things that have changed you

your eyes are half closed because
you are still laying there
in bed
vulnerable
and your arms sprawled out
with pieces of lint from the sheets on your cheek

I want you to be the first thing you thought of
when you made it out of your own mind

I want to hear you say good morning before the day
takes you down its unpredictable winding roads

tell me,
would that mean I have conquered you-
my love?

tell your daughters

when the world laughs at me
I know it is because I am different
complex
contradictory
eclectic
and on a road of my own

I have learned that in order to be myself
there must be an element of fearlessness

there must be the ability to go through unmentionable things
and survive
there must be a crooked road conquered
a story to tell

in a world of sheep
I dare to be the wolf

I dare to love and be loved
I dare to lose love and not lose myself

when you were there

I thought love was me picking your towels off of the floor
and reaching for you after a long day

I thought love was when you would buy me medicine and fold up my socks and
headscarves

I thought it was when you would wake me up to tea and stories on the news

yes

that is what I thought love was all this time
the small things

the things that will haunt you the most

temples

inside of me there are writings on the walls
but there are no intruders allowed
only someone who will walk softly
and watch their step on the way in
wash your past lovers off your skin before entering
we can't have uninvited spirits moving around us
taunting us about our past
and all the lips we've kissed

my body can be a temple for you and for me
but no burdens are allowed here
only love
black tea
and bamboos

only your mouth on mine
and your words dancing around
dripping slowly like sap from a tree
lingering throughout the day

inside of me there are writings on the walls
and sun and moon
a place where you can plant yourself

newspapers

there are times when I read an article from the paper to you in the mornings just to see your expressions. there are bombs going off. there are mothers drowning their children. there is war outside. but from our view we can only see our linens on the clothing line, blowing in the wind, delicately.

i watch your eyebrows. to see if they rise. i look to see if sorrow makes your mouth go downward. i look to your body language to see if it hardens or trembles. does it provoke something inside of you? does it make you want to protect or surrender?

there is the world outside and then there is us. but you were once outside of us and so was i.

i watch you. i am searching for the softness within you.

i need to know that you are not still made of wars.

daughters of rolling stones part 2

i have learned to do all of those things
without the presence of a man in the home
we fixed things with our little hands
we bandaged ourselves
got mud on the bottom of our dresses
raking leaves
cutting weeds
taking trash
fixing beds and doors

I have watched a woman do all of these things
they say a man does
with her fragile nurturing body in the yard
working
cutting grass

my mother

coming in, then cutting fruit
for the pies
a sip of wine
the job is done
and starts again

I have learned all of these things
so when you say
I do not know how to let you be a man

I want to please you
but

I have learned so many things
with my fragile hands

intuition

when you say that I am nothing
I am still breasts that feed
and body that grows life
I am mother nature personified
and articulated

when you toss me away

I know that God is not in you

medusa rising

if there are snakes in my hair and flowers in my hands
it is only because I have been traveling

if you must dehumanize me
because now I appear wild and dangerous
then you must not know

where long dirt roads will take you
when you are vulnerable
and searching

you find just what you were looking for
because desperation is dew on your skin
it drips
and leaves trails behind you

and there you stand
being eaten alive
by men
like vultures

all because you wanted love
tucked underneath you
when you returned

ripe

she isn't delicate
she's cognac
a pebble in your boot
she's lonely as the trees
forgotten

ripened fruit

doves part 2

for the first time she felt lovely
and refused to look in any mirrors to confirm it

before,
she was riding in cars with men
who saw her mouth a cracked mountain
a hole
to throw things into-
murky waters
lies
their own broken spirits

now,
her spirit is burning sage
recalculating itself
it is sweeping away the handprints of past lovers
from her skin and inner thigh
the blood inside of them now echo
how she is almond milk sustenance

and mountain for mouth
blessed to swallow a past made of moths
and spit out exploding moons and red seas

non political

I am not punishing men when I let the hair on my body grow
or when I cut off all of my hair

i am not punishing myself
or trying to make any overt statements

it is far from political
it is simply comfort
acceptance

but the comfort is not long lived
because it is ingrained

to be inorganic

to be what they want and when
to give until there is nothing left

east of a cold red sun

life occurs in flashes
flashing lessons across the lenses of your eyes
flapping into your ears
the sound of it
creates flavors for you to taste
and decipher what is poison

and there you are
closing your eyes to dim the lighting
listening to things that block everything else out
the things that tell you who to be
how to think

the things that take away from the gifts that come
from when you live
and when you are still

the ways of the mountains
the ways of the east

secrets in the cabinets

when will your aunts and grandmothers stop sweeping?
sweeping the secrets under the rugs
protecting men in the family
perverse in their ways
looking
and lifting your clothing
in dark corners
with hands
that stick
leaving you wondering if God was watching

when the coffee brews early
and the night is finally gone
there is tension in the floors you walk across
because the walls whisper
shame

the night you can never hide from

and you are told to be silent
or else
you will hurt everyone

and you can see the cabinets rattle

and there you are, a silent weeping sore
that people pick when they pass by

and your aunts offer ointments
and your mother's a blind eye

and the future holds
resilience

or the need
to forever numb

swept up secrets

furthermore

there is something about the way you speak
honesty comes leaping out
stories from your childhood hang pictures

and I am an open hole
hurrying it inside
because I am more hungry
for honesties
than anything else I have ever known

things fall apart

I like lovers with wisdom in their hands
so that their touch is familiar but strange enough
to feel pristine

I like lovers who split themselves open and say,
this is who I am –
is this okay?

I like lovers who have scars in the same places as I
who have sat in the same dark rooms pacing
trying to figure out things that will never make sense

who have had the same conversations
with strangers
about why things fall apart

they do not believe in magic
they believe in the seasons
because they have tasted each one
and at times
found themselves betrayed
when they were cold in summer
and mountainless in the fall

I like lovers who have regret in their skin
lessons that have created soft lines around the eyes

eyes that remind you of a place you have been to
but cannot recall where
you just know you were younger
and more immortal then

I like lovers that speak boldly
but gain softness towards the end
because they read your body language
the way your hands fidget

reading between the lines of your palms
and your truths that have ran you ragged

wives and lace in the bayou

we went down to the bayou
with our lace
and naked legs
to talk in languages of motherhood
to talk about our husbands
and how they so often strayed
and how our skin was starting to dry
becoming stiffer
and unwelcoming

we would talk about new table cloths
and potato gardens
and cellulite

we would rub frothy moss against it
because the witch doctors say it gives skin youth

we would walk slowly back home
to finish making bread

trying to please mother nature
before our men
before ourselves

humming

i would speak softly
and the men would say how much they adored it

I would speak softly
and the women would yell for me to speak up

I am still trying to appease them both

I am still trying to figure out who to appease first

orange dresses

one day you won't overwhelm my senses

and I will ask you to go with me to East Africa
to pick coffee beans

to put sand that breathes
underneath our feet

we will love there
burn sage there
decorate balconies there
become one there

conquer me there

underneath my dress
turn my body into falling rain

violet part 1

whatever violet wants
violet gets

with long lovely bones
and eyes that burn you alive

they never let her go
no
they always returned

but they were taught not to love women like her

only soft ones
who would ignore their transgressions

for the sake of white dresses
church bells

societal accolades

the story of balconies

there's a haze outside that seems to be waiting for what-ifs. I can't hear the music over your smile or your drunken 'I love you' confessions. and your hands are pulling me outside to the balcony where the air feels like silk, to hear you talk about your sister who lives on a different coast. and your favorite museums. you laugh as you slip and fall.

and I just want to fall with you. and make mistake after mistake. take my vacancy sign down. and lay down welcome mats.

nobody seems to be watching. everybody is inside laughing and dancing and some of them found their way downstairs and are not engulfed in talking conspiracies.

and here we are. studying each other's faces. we're made of hieroglyphics and west side stories. you're looking for a green light and I'm looking for eyes I can trust.

on a night like this

where it's all about mistakes
slips
and falls

after talks about museums that touch something different inside of you.

must be the sun

open your eyes
there is a light piercing through
the darkness that sunk into your bones
for over a decade

there are slits in your skin
that have turned to pink from grey
and flowers are sprouting from them

speaking to the sun

saying amen
saying ase

renegades

don't you love how she leaves something behind each time she runs out the door? to let you know she will always return and fall into you after the world has showed her she does not belong there without you? without your scent blooming from her skin?

classics

you want to love one part of me and not the other
but
you'll be needing that other part after a while

to light a fire
or even to bring some rain

when you are a drought
when the world refuses to understand you

put flowers in my hair

taste me
drink me
love me
put flowers in my hair
forgive my past
paint me
lead me
follow me
paint my soul lilac
put me in a frame
high above a fireplace
or a black mountain that brushes heaven
when the wind blows

whisper things that put me back together

put me back together again

purple ties (grandfather)

my grandfather is the greatest man I've ever known
there are lessons to be learned in his silence

and his woodsheds

wisdom sits at his feet
waiting for inquiry
in the evenings

after he can no longer busy himself
with the day

and in the distance
there are lions, tigers, and bears

but he is never afraid

full

I want a love that seeps into my pores and sticks to my bones

I want to be filled to the brim with it

happily drowning

corridors

sometimes I feel my heart creaking like old doors
and I wonder how it will feel after another ten years
if I keep letting love in and out

blackbird sings

you are a blackbird
with happiness
that smudges beneath you

you have learned how to create happiness
you have learned how to nurture it within you
even when sadness is dripping
all around you

even when your heart feels a thousand years old

tell your daughters part 2

the biggest thing I have learned is to live unedited
unapologetically
to yell this is who I am
and to tell the anxiety that comes with it
it will never win

there is nothing more freeing in life
than to be who you are
and to be who you were meant to be

there is nothing more empowering
than acknowledging your weaknesses
and your strengths

and saying

this is what I am

and this is why

my story is my own

songs for the oppressed

we are going to walk forward
even if the world spits its venom on us
and tells us we were meant to fail

we do not need validation
we know who we are
and we know we were born to be warriors
if need be

our words will be spears
our determination ammunition
our knowledge, hand grenades

splitting oppressors between the eyes

we will stand in place
and take back
everything they have taken

red china

when I cook for you
I use red china
and use your grandmother's recipes

when we're sitting in the backyard
listening to crickets and trees

I can see myself giving you sons

the earth sits still
and in that moment
i could die

in that moment
happiness explodes
silently

and you don't even know it
because words could never express

but tears
tears could

black flowers
black feathers
drifting upward to a delicate blue sky could

anything terrifyingly beautiful
could

red sun rising

I have learned how to stay up late
and out all night
to keep my mind off of things that leech

but it returns in the morning
carrying baskets of ashes

telling me how love tastes at different hours

the grand exit

why do you feel the need to tell me you still love me
when you were afraid before
and jumped ship
faster than
the sun
could set

I am not the type of person who sits by
twiddling my thumbs

making habits out of love
mocking the one thing that mankind does recklessly
without fail

you were afraid
not me

I do not need to hear about your cowardly love
I do not know its language

guitars in the art shed

there's a collection of songs
that bounce off of the walls
and twirl up into the air
like cigar smoke
it loops and circles
and I inhale
and set it loose

there's a love that drags on like guitar strings
and I need you here

pretending
if you must

make my sky line hum
electricity

I just need you.
I just need you to stay forever.

purpose in collisions

there are wars within my skin
trying to find its place
raging
sputtering
then still

there are wars within my feet
wailing
with stories
folding
aching

there are wars within my words
contradicting
biting
scratching
then silent

I am exhausted but it is not in vain
these wars set the stage
for calm

it takes strength to find your peace in the end
it takes strength to find purpose in the collisions
because none of us can escape the wars inside of us

lolita

when your hands are pressed against mine
I envision long fields
full of water

and honeysuckles under a rising sun
slowly twirling

I can't imagine the things I would see
if you were to do much more

if your breath were to touch mine
if your eyes were to trust mine

if no one ever had to know
so that it could never be ruined

all known things get so beautifully ruined

papa's karma

I am so sorry I brought you here
to be burned alive by love
to have angst within your skin
and earth that does not cater
to the softness or the journeys of your feet

to have ridiculous ideals to live up to
to stretch yourself thin
just to live up to what is expected

but you are already not what is expected

and can you hear that?
rejection, even from other women, beating
down your door
and swimming in the sinks

I am so sorry
there is no way out
now that you are here
I will sharpen you the best I can
so that you cannot crumble
even when crumbling is what's best
because you are a woman
made to fold

because you were designed to love until
there nothing is left of you

vases

I saw my angry orchid turn into dark angry knots
greying over in its vase

it later blossomed in a dark corner
after being mistaken for dead

and I thought to myself
what if I could do the same?

and I did
just the same

the reminder

find yourself
and don't let yourself go
after you find what it was
that you were looking for
within

and make a promise not to lose yourself
again

if

if no one has told you,
you are deserving of a love
that looks like art
that is art

if no one has told you,
your broken parts look like art
the way they are all tangled up like strings

they are art

your experiences have molded you
to fit into this world
but to seem as though you are not of this world

you could be where the soft or wild things are

you are magnificent and imperfect
the light at the very end of the darkest day

the light everyone seeks

to create the perfect thing

story of cold floors

I have been aching in odd places over the course of 100 days. I have been attracting men who have blood of papaya fruits and honey dripping from their mouths. they speak syrupy sweet lies that bite like mosquitos.

I hid in my room and took down the mirrors. if only because I was disappointed in myself for believing any of the things they had said.

the healer said that an old lover had left spirits inside of me, swimming, tangling itself up. he wondered if there were any thorns piercing through my skin from the inside. sometimes, the spirits try to get out. he said everyone should protect themselves from spirits of old lovers.

I was waking up in the middle of the night with a dull ache inside my throat as if I was dying. as if I had smoked a thousand cigarettes. an ache inside my legs, as if I had been bitten by a thousand lions.

I went to the witch doctor in the bayou. she ordered 25 healing crystals.

I laid on the cold bare floor and lay them over me. I put one over each eye, to block out re-occurring dreams of abandonment that manifested as visuals of fire in the sky and raging vultures circling.

I woke up with breathing bones. I woke up hollow. I was an echoing thing.

how could it be that I was more frightening than before?

black moon

today I will taste joy
even if it might be just a slice

today
I will travel to places
where there are no roads
or weeping willows
that don't sit upright

today I will sleep in beds of flowers
and linens hanging from trees

today I will write letters
to those I have forgiven
but still linger in passing thoughts

today
I will manifest the joy
of sun rays
beaming over slanted hills

today a black swan
flies
away

mistresses in the bayou

there was black lace covering her hands. to match her bedding next to the vase of fresh cut flowers, from the garden, she cut with perfect nails. for him to smell. when he came. kissing her and planting sorrows in her lips. inside her walls. pulling ribbons from between her legs. while she stood on her arched feet. to breathe him in. before he leaves. a lonely sting.

soft wild things

there are places, where soft wild things explode. where they chase the moon
and cold red sun. where love never dies. where every inch of your body drips like a sap
tree, when your lover reaches inside of you. and stays there forever, as if your body was
God.

kept woman

if I had known that you would never marry me
I would have never met your mother
in a classic vintage gown with white gloves
and a soft voice
that rang like a church bell gripped tightly

I would have painted my lips red instead
I would have made my heart a foreign place
full of velvet languages
that made you smash up walls
because you could not learn them

mexico

he wanted me to go with him past the borders
where the sky looks crumbled up
be the one who could get him in heaven
forget who I was before

he wanted to ride me around
love only him
not make a sound
forget who I was before

he wanted to ruin me
make me of no use to anyone else
because he never loved such a sweet fragile thing

he wanted our worlds to end
along the coast
that day

forget who I was before

I found a love

I found a lover who puts beads on strings and sews me up
he sews me up around my hands
across the wrist
into the belly
I found a lover who wants to stay a while

his mama must be made of fruit trees

.

generational curses

I was wanting to try again but I had no room left for the unspeakable pain of the things they say are inevitable. things like divorce, infidelity, or widowhood.

I advised myself long ago to insulate my insides with petals of violets so love could never quite slice like a sword. but, what if it became a hurricane, breaking me up. scattering things around. making stories out of me.

curses can swim. curses can be winds. curses can be stones. rolling.

bound

come fly
there are no winds here to steer you east
when you want to go west
come love
where there are no curses
for the sins of fathers or mothers
come be
where the dark is as sweet as the light
where bliss tastes like grapefruits
and it settles under the sun
soft and wild
bound to self-love
decorated in sage and moon skin

never going home

when my sister speaks, her breath smells of cherry colas
and vanillas
they all come crashing down
in love with her
nestling themselves against her
trying to twirl her hair
with their fingers

trying to pluck violets from her skin

lighthouse

when you say you love me
I cannot hear you
there's jazz playing
Billie Holiday
so I say, oh not now, love

there are lake waters outside
brushing up against the side of our home
like a storm
looking for its long lost love

so when I say I love you too
you can't hear me either
there's a pot whistling
and photos along the floor
that seem to say, not now, dove

aren't lighthouses a gloomy sight?
didn't you learn about fleeting love from your mother?
won't this fleeting moments of us get you high anyhow
because it reminds you of old storms?

blood in the dirt

I will not sit in your red huts
and dust my knees
or arch my feet for hours
and bleed into dirt
for your comfort
or your watchful eye
I am not shame
I am creator
the home for seed
and birth
womb of what is coming

i will sprawl myself out onto the floor
and send you out
so I can let mother nature
recharge me
and turn me into a tree of life

you can go into that hut, if you are the one who is afraid of magic remnants

I will never be jealous of any lover you find who reaped the fruits of my labor. the beauty of it all is that, my last memory of you is grasping, as it all slipped through your hands. I taught you how to love. I taught you what love lost tastes like. the bitter taste.

it never quite goes away.

that is the beauty in labor that went without fruit for so long.

clinging

if I am strong, you say it is unattractive
if I am independent, that is unattractive too

the only thing I want from you is the love of a thousand moons

but when I ask for that, you will say I am a leech that clings
and you want out

so who are you to dismiss my ability to rise on my own
or my ability to understand that love requires a woman of strength
who knows it is a clinging thing

unfolding

I love to see how you unfold so softly
when I look at you and say, hey love
you become a protector
a love without one weeping sore
a love that breaks up things from the past that try to hold me hostage

pyramid

be swift
write your truth
or throw colors on a blank canvas
every story that has caused you heartache
and made you who you are
manifest it in creativity
then be free

our girls

there are girls running to get away from wars
and guns so loud
they urinate themselves
they drip trauma
while murky waters
wrap around their legs

there are soldiers in their land, taking them
mutilating them
raping them
murdering them

so they run
from village to village
for safety
but finding none

this is happening
in modern day

but their piercing cries fall on deafened ears

there will be karma for the silence

*why do we
do nothing*

story of barbwire

sorry is not enough. sometimes

 it is just

not enough.

that is what I heard my mother yell at him, as she tumbled over her foot and down the stairs. her pin curls were draping down, frizzing, making other plans. she slammed the door and it was so silent you could hear the black birds landing in the fields.
I looked out into the gray sky and heard the sudden sound of gravel under tires. then rocks flying against the window. the final battle cry of goodbye.
she took her robe and threw it at the foot of the stairs and nearly collapsed at the silence. once she noticed I was watching, she motioned me over with a lopsided smile and cradled me into her sides. there was a crinkle around her eye I had not seen before. she smiled and kissed my cheek with soft burgundy lips that felt like a single feather from one of those blackbirds outside. I could see veins popping from her hands. it looked like barbwire. it was as if she had been griping something that would never budge or sit upright.
she had been thrown into the sky and left to fall, but there was no shattered glass here. there was only a tightness in her jaw, that looked like a small raging ball of flesh. a ball that would burst later behind closed doors when "I am sorry" would replay itself, but not be enough.
when it became so silent, all she could hear was the wind moving the gravel back into place or her pin curl falling.

body languages of old souls

there is a wind in your eyes. your story seems to propel that wind. it seems eager for me
to inquire. to get lost in it. and understand why you are. smudged around the edges. or
how you survived. when no one cared. if you lived. or if you breathed. almost as if
it knows I will understand. as if my eyes are bandages. or a water basin.

remember
pain does not last always
and when you try to numb it with things
or people
it will still be waiting for you to come back home

I need to face it
dont run

remember
there are small victories that you have forgotten
that you have won on your own
that make you powerful
when you only thought you were weak

do not forget who you want to become
do not forget the universe created you to be exactly who you are

so be

remember
love lost cannot destroy you
if you allow it to be a lesson instead

You will be a lesson for me
that I never could have taught myself

remember
there is always a lesson
in it all

a late entry

conquer
it is ok to be vulnerable. it is ok to grieve, cry and mourn. it is ok to say I am not ok. it is ok to plant yourself in a dark corner until you feel that there is light. we often do not allow ourselves to find peace the right way. we force our eyes to be dry when they should release tears. we smile and laugh when we really want to frown and hide. we dance when we really want to fall to the floor to cry.

we function. we show strength. we do what is expected, except be human and allow ourselves to feel.

how can we ever really be strong when we take away the moments that make us strong? the moments meant to give wisdom? the moments that are meant to teach.

life is unpredictable. there is pain and loss. there is heartache, death, divorce, humiliation, and trauma. there are moments that rip us to shreds. there are moments where you wonder if you would be better off- no longer on this earth. some situations cause us to go to deep dark places. we beat ourselves up for being there. we paint ourselves as failures because we dared to feel. we dared to ache until we throbbed.

the dark places lead to the light.

life is balance of the two.

we must lick our wounds. we must use our hands to apply ointments to the wounds. we must learn that ointment is time. time to grieve. time to heal. time to gather. and time to let go.

we must always eventually let go of the pain. when the time is right you will feel the nudge. you will feel as though you have blossomed through dry cracked dirt.

we must crawl towards happiness and scrape our skin along the way.

we must search for it and claim it as our own.

Thank you.

Bio:

www.shataraliora.com

Inquiries:
iamshataraliora@gmail.com

Made in the USA
Lexington, KY
15 July 2017